The Magic of
Forests

Written and illustrated by
Vicky Woodgate

Contents

DK | Penguin Random House

Author and Illustrator Vicky Woodgate
Concept and Design Vicky Woodgate

Editor Kathleen Teece
US Senior Editor Shannon Beatty
US Editor Mindy Fichter
Consultant Mark Rayment
Jacket Designer Sonny Flynn
Managing Editor Jonathan Melmoth
Managing Art Editor Diane Peyton Jones
Production Editor Dragana Puvacic
Production Controller Inderjit Bhullar
Publishing Director Sarah Larter

First American Edition, 2023
Published in the United States by DK Publishing
1745 Broadway, 20th Floor, New York, NY 10019

Text and illustrations Copyright Vicky Woodgate

23 24 25 26 27 10 9 8 7 6 5 4 3 2 1
001-336097-Aug/2023

A catalog record for this book
is available from the Library of Congress.
ISBN 978-0-7440-8310-1

DK books are available at special discounts when purchased
in bulk for sales promotions, premiums, fund-raising, or educational
use. For details, contact: DK Publishing Special Markets,
1745 Broadway, 20th Floor, New York, NY 10019
SpecialSales@dk.com

Printed and bound in China

For the curious
www.dk.com

MIX
Paper | Supporting
responsible forestry
FSC™ C018179

This book was made with Forest
Stewardship Council™ certified
paper – one small step in DK's
commitment to a sustainable future.
For more information go to
www.dk.com/our-green-pledge

The BIGGEST
tree hugging
session had
4,620 huggers!

What is a forest?

Feline forestry fan

This is Mimi cat. She will lead us on a fabulous journey through the amazing world of all things forest. After all, cats LOVE to climb trees.

So, what IS a forest? Well, it's not just a bunch of trees! A forest is a VERY important ecosystem. It houses all sorts of life—plants big and small, fungi, and a menagerie of weird and wonderful animals and insects.

The trees clean the air by making oxygen for us to breathe and sucking in gases that cause climate change. There are forest creatures that would make the mind boggle—and we haven't discovered them all yet! In the darkest depths of the world's forests, new marvels are found every day. Now, let's check out all the different forest types (yep, there are more than just one kind) and see what astonishing things we can discover.

Woodlands, forests, jungles

What IS the difference?

All three have trees with plants growing in between. But their treetop layers, or canopies, let in more or less light, and one has a floor covered in tangled plants. Read on to learn which is which.

BY ROYAL DECREE

The medieval kings of Europe LOVED to hunt. And they didn't want people destroying the homes of their quarry, such as boar. So, hunting lands were renamed "royal forests," where damaging trees and killing animals was punished. In the 11th century, a whopping one-third of England's land was royal forest!

25–60%

of a woodland is covered by a tree canopy.

Red squirrel

10 MILLION

At 50 years old, oak trees start producing their nuts, which are called acorns. An oak tree can make more than 10 million acorns in its lifetime. Only a few acorns will grow into new trees, the rest will become food for woodland creatures.

Woodland

A woodland is usually planted or managed (cared for) in some way. It has less canopy cover than a forest, which means more light reaches the ground. Lots of ground-dwelling creatures, such as deer and rabbits, love woodlands.

Red admiral

Horsefly

Little brown bat

THE TALLEST

Hyperion, a giant redwood, is thought to be the tallest tree in the world. It lives in a forest in the Redwood National Park in California. At 380 ft (116 m), it is taller than the Statue of Liberty in New York City.

Purple emperor

Nuthatch

60–100%

of a forest is covered by a tree canopy.

Forests

A forest can be managed or wild. It is more packed with trees than a woodland, with more canopy cover. This means less light reaches the ground. Tree-dwelling animals, such as squirrels, owls, pine martens, woodpeckers, and bobcats, thrive in the forest trees.

Deer sometimes hide their babies in the dense undergrowth.

Fawn

Swinging

Jungles have thick vines called lianas. Many animals that live high up in the trees use them to travel by swinging from one tree to another. That must be so much fun!

Jungles

Jungles are not managed, which means they are packed full of plants that cover the floor and grow up tree trunks. They are found in hot, wet parts of the world. Amazing animals can be found in jungles—some have become the stars of books and films, such as *Tarzan* and *The Jungle Book*.

Green tree python

100%

of a jungle is covered by many layers of canopy.

A VERY STINKY FLOWER

In the jungles of Indonesia grows the largest and smelliest flower in the world. Its dead-animal stench earned it the name "corpse flower"—ewww!

Stinking corpse lily

Carrion flies

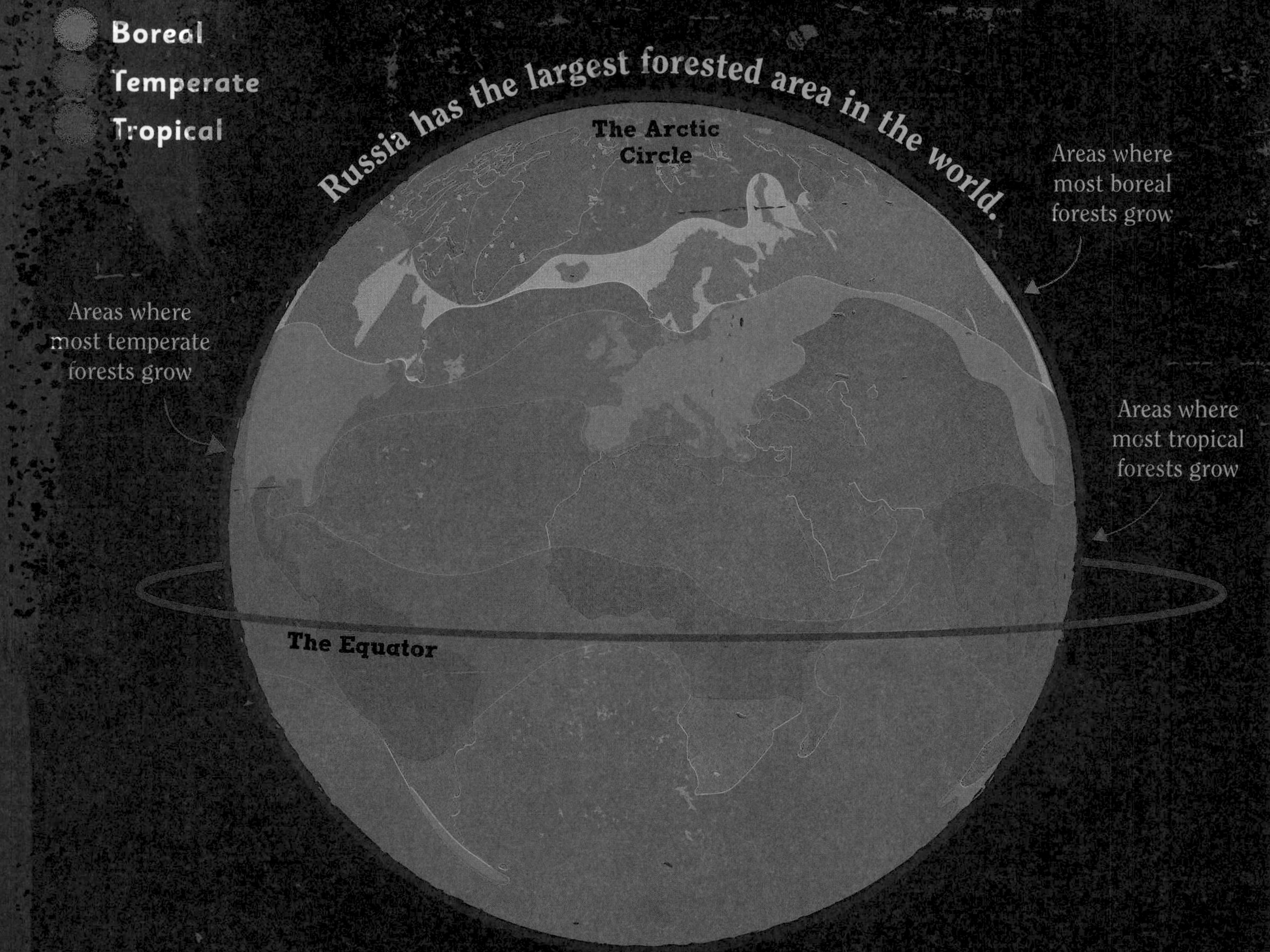

Boreal
Temperate
Tropical

Russia has the largest forested area in the world.

The Arctic
Circle

Areas where
most boreal
forests grow

Areas where
most temperate
forests grow

Areas where
most tropical
forests grow

The Equator

80%
of all land animals
live in forests.

30%
of the Earth's land is
covered by forest.

Types
of forests

There are three main types of forests—boreal, temperate,
and tropical. Where they are in the world, and what kind of
weather they have, plays a big part in what type of forest they
are. Boreal, or taiga, forests rarely reach temperatures above
freezing. Temperate forests have four distinct seasons. Tropical
forests are the hottest and wettest—and the most full of life.

4 seasons

There are long, harsh winters, short, bright summers, and fleeting springs and falls.

Boreal

Boreal forests are packed with conifer trees. They form a band below the Arctic Circle through Asia, Europe, and North America. The winters are extremely cold and can last eight months. Then there is a growing period of around four months, when trees shoot upward in long, light-filled summer days.

Plants

Pines, spruce, larch, and fir trees fill boreal forests, along with some deciduous trees (trees that lose their leaves in winter), such as birch and aspen. Blueberries and other fruit shrubs crowd the forest floor, along with fungi, mosses, lichens, and cute, flowering sundews. A few plants are carnivorous (meat-eating)—the purple pitcher feasts on insects.

Wildlife

Some truly iconic creatures call these most northern forests home. There are wolverines, moose, bears, wolves, foxes, huge owls, and even a species of tiger—the Siberian, or Amur. Many birds fly south in winter to warmer climates, where food still grows.

BOREAL FOREST STRUCTURE

CANOPY	Dominated by needle-leaved conifers, and some broad-leaved, deciduous hardwoods
UNDERSTORY	Short, woody shrubs
FOREST FLOOR	Plenty of lichens and mosses
SOIL	Moist, with not much nutrients, host to shallow roots

30%

of the world's forests are boreal.

Canadian warbler

ANCIENT EVERGREENS

Pine trees usually have a life span of 100–1,000 years—however the oldest known pine is nearly 5,000 years old! These trees are evergreen, which means they keep their leaves all year round. There are more of them than any other coniferous tree, split into around 115 different species.

Boreal chorus frog

Siberian tiger

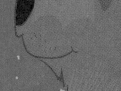

Grizzly bear

9

TEMPERATE FOREST STRUCTURE

Dominated by deciduous trees	CANOPY
Shrubs and younger trees	UNDERSTORY
Mosses, fungi, ferns, and flowers	FOREST FLOOR
Moist and rich in nutrients, host to shallow roots	SOIL

Temperate

Broad-leaved trees rule in these forests. They can be found between the tropics (the zones either side of the equator) and the polar regions (the areas at the very top and bottom of the Earth). Their busy year includes four wildly different seasons. Temperate rainforests are a unique environment—as wet as other rainforests, but with much milder temperatures.

4 seasons

Winters are mild, summers are warm, spring is wet, and fall is crisp—with leaves turning incredible, fiery colors.

SUPER SOIL

The temperate forest floor is very fertile (which means a lot of things grow). Fallen leaves that litter the ground break down into nutrients that other plants—as well as fungi—can take in to help them grow. And, of course, more plants and fungi means more food for small critters.

European hedgehog

25%

of global forests are temperate.

Pileated woodpecker

Tree bumblebee

Plants

The most common trees here are beech, oak, maple, and chestnut. Most of the trees are broad-leaved and will lose their leaves in winter. Lichens, mosses, ferns, shrubs, and wildflowers also thrive.

Wildlife

Some of the animals you might spot in temperate forests are deer, badgers, boar, chipmunks, foxes, woodpeckers, owls, frogs, and salamanders. And there are plenty of insects, too—including bees, butterflies, and moths. The creatures here can cleverly adapt to survive the weather changes throughout the year.

1 or 2 seasons

Some tropical forests have two seasons—rainy and dry—while tropical rainforests have rainy, humid weather all year round.

PRECIOUS FORESTS

Rainforests cover six percent of our planet's surface, but are home to around half of all its plants and animals. Plants thrive in this moist, sunny part of the world, providing animals with homes and plenty of food.

Plants

170,000 of the 250,000 plant species in existence can be found in tropical rainforests. There are banana and rubber trees, orchids, and cacao—which is what chocolate is made from! Tropical rainforests have different trees, depending on where they are. In Africa, you might stumble across the thorny acacia, while bamboo and sandalwood grow in India.

Tropical

In the areas just above and below the equator exist forests that are warm all year round. Some of these forests are rainforests—which are lush, green, and packed with life. More than half of all known life on Earth can be found in this type of tropical forest.

Potoo

TROPICAL FOREST STRUCTURE

OVERSTORY	The tops of very tall trees
CANOPY	Home to plenty of plants and animals
UNDERSTORY	Full of palms and vines
FOREST FLOOR	Very dark, with little sunlight.
SOIL	Acidic and low in nutrients

Bullet ants

45% of global forests are tropical.

Green vine snake

Wildlife

Here, there are countless colorful tree frogs, vibrant parrots, slow-moving sloths, swinging monkeys, and cats, such as mysterious panthers. There are also ants—everywhere. In fact, there are over 200 types of ants. A mind-boggling variety of wildlife!

Red-eyed tree frog

Sloth (in a hat)

Family tree groups

All modern trees are called spermatophores, and reproduce (make new trees) using seeds. Spermatophores can be split into two groups. These are...

Gymnosperms

Nonflowering trees are called gymnosperms. They have female cones, which need pollen from male cones to be able to grow seeds. Some examples are conifers, such as pine, and cycads, which have crowns of long leaves.

Angiosperms

These are flowering trees with seeds that grow inside fruit. Angiosperm trees lose their leaves in fall and regrow them in spring. Most trees are within this group.

An oak is an angiosperm.

Oak tree

Leaves

Branches

What is a tree?

A tree is a type of shrub (a plant with a woody stem, or stems). It usually has a single stem, called a trunk, which does not die in winter. There are around 64,000 named species of trees, and more yet to be discovered! Some are huge, growing taller than houses. Others are smaller than pencils.

Trunk

A sturdy trunk grows up from the ground. It connects the roots in the soil below to the branches and leaves up top. Some species have more than one trunk, and are called multi-stemmed trees.

Trunk

Flowers

Canopy

Fruits

Nuts are
fruits, too!

AMAZING OAK

An oak tree can support a whopping
2,300 species of microbes, insects, and
animals in its lifetime. It can grow up to
76 ft (23 m) high—that's the equivalent of
four giraffes on top of each other! Some
oaks can live 1,000 years, or more.

Flowers and fruits

Plants need pollen to make seeds. This
is both made by flowers and collected
by them—usually from visiting insects,
who have it stuck to their bodies. Fruits
are a way to spread seeds so that they
have space to grow. Fruits are eaten by
animals, and the seeds come out in
droppings elsewhere. Smart!

Branches

These grow outward and upward
from the trunk. Twigs grow from the
branches, and leaves, flowers, and
fruits or nuts sprout from the twigs.
Water and food pass to different
parts of the tree through branches.

Bark

Leaves

These are full of chlorophyll—a green
chemical that gives them their usual
color. Chlorophyll helps leaves absorb
sunlight, which trees use to make the
energy they need to grow. So, leaves
are sort of like solar panels!

Bark

This tough outer layer surrounds
the trunk. It protects the tree from
the weather, invading insects, fire,
and disease. Some animals have strong
enough teeth to eat bark, such as
squirrels, monkeys, and beavers.

Roots

Beaver

The tree is anchored to the ground with roots. But
that's not their only job—they also spread out
through the soil in search of food and water.

Fruity

A mushroom is only one part of a fungus—it is the fruiting body that makes spores. Below ground, fungi can stretch on and on!

Tree root

Ants

Hello!

There's food here.

Mother trees

Older plants (mother trees) use their deeper root systems to get more nutrients for younger plants nearby that need a little help. And dying trees can send their own food reserves out to their neighbors.

I feel sick.

Earthworm

Talking forest

Under the forest floor, a secret conversation is taking place between plants. A network of tiny fungal threads connects plants and allows them to swap food and information, creating a connection that can span entire forests. The threads are made by fungi, to find sugary food and water—which is what they get from plugging into plant roots. In return, the trees get nutrients from the fungi. It's a win-win!

Mushroom

Hyphae

I'm hungry!

I'm thirsty.

More than mushrooms

The living body of the fungus is called a mycelium. It is made up of a web of tiny little threads, which are called hyphae (hi-fee).

What ARE fungi?

These unique life-forms are closer to animals than to plants. They have their very own kingdom, with millions of different types. And we haven't discovered all of them yet!

Dung beetle

Helpful critters

Worms break down organic (living or once-living) matter, such as leaves, into nutrients that fungi and plants can take in. The burrowing tunnels of worms and other creatures also help water flow through the soil, for plants and fungi to drink up.

Fungal friends

Some fungi are diseases for plants—but others are friendly. These helpful fungi are called mycorrhizae (my-cor-rye-zee). It is the mycorrhizae that create a network with plant roots, which is sometimes called the wood wide web.

Mole

15

Leaf detective

Each leaf is one of hundreds of different shapes around the world, which might make it tricky to know which tree it came from! But, luckily for us detectives, leaves fall into two main categories—broadleaves and needles or scales. And we can narrow it down further than that...

Rounded lobes

Some simple leaves have lobes—rounded and pointed segments around the edge.

The maple leaf is a simple structure. It has three or more lobes with jagged, sawlike edges.

Pointed lobes

Oak leaf

Maple leaf

Toothed edges

Compound structures have a lot of leaflets attached to the stem, such as on this horse chestnut leaf.

Horse chestnut leaf

Broadleaves

There are two types of broadleaves—simple and compound. A simple leaf structure has only one blade (leaf), which is attached to a twig by its stem. A compound structure has two or more blades, which are attached to a middle stem coming off a twig. The shape and edges on broadleaves vary a lot. Some are smooth, some have sharp teeth, and some even look like hands!

A beech leaf has a simple structure. It is oval-shaped with a tip and smooth, wavy edges.

The palm is a compound leaf. It has many swordlike leaflets.

Beech leaf

Palm leaf

16

Needle leaves are long and thin.

Pine leaves

Needles and scales

Needlelike and scaly leaves are found on many conifers—cone-producing trees, such as pines, spruces, and firs. Many are green all year round.

Cypress leaf

Scaly leaves have tiny, overlapping structures on flat branchlets.

Veins

Inside a broadleaf are many little veins. They work like blood vessels, carrying water and food throughout the plant. Needle leaves only have one vein running from the top to the bottom.

Veins

LITTLE AND LARGE

The biggest tree leaf in the world is on a raffia palm called the Raphia regalis. Each leaf can reach a whopping 82 ft (25 m) long—the length of three London buses! The smallest tree leaf grows on the tiny dwarf willow. This tree can be as little as 0.4 in (1 cm) tall. Imagine how tiny the leaves are!

Quiz

Do these questions stump you?

1. What is the top layer of a tropical forest called?

   a. Understory
   b. Overstory
   c. Canopy

2. Do you know how many species of pine trees there are?

   a. 110
   b. 115
   c. 120

3. What are jungle vines called?

   a. Llamas
   b. Bananas
   c. Lianas

4. Which country has the most forested areas in the world?

   a. Canada
   b. China
   c. Russia

5. How many acorns can an ancient oak produce in its lifetime?

   a. 5 billion
   b. 10 million
   c. 1 trillion

Answers: 1. b, 2. b, 3. c, 4. c, 5. b

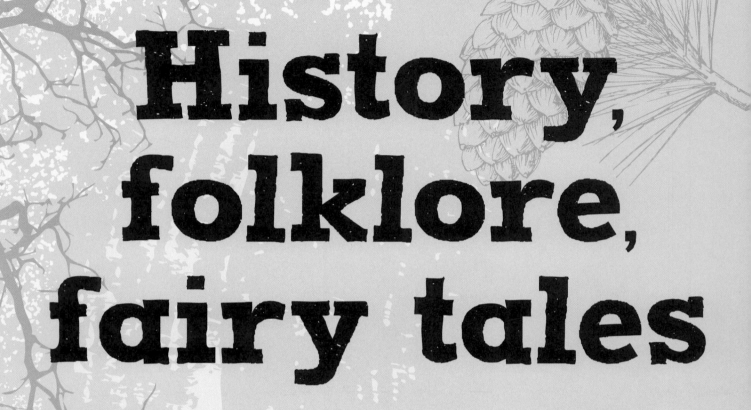

History, folklore, fairy tales

Fairy cats

A mythical Norwegian fairy cat was said to be too huge and fluffy to pick up. In fact, the stories were describing the adorable Norwegian Forest cat! Meow!

The first forests grew up nearly
400 million years ago. They have survived mass
extinctions, giant, plant-munching dinosaurs,
asteroids, and freezing ice ages, brrrrr...

Since the earliest civilizations, these wild,
tangled places have inspired many otherworldly
tales. Dark shadows, eerie sounds, and the
whisper of wind through the trees—surely, they
must be enchanted? Ancient stories tell
of witches, gods, spirits, unicorns,
fairies, elves, and ghosts.

Dark and dangerous, magical and mysterious, do
we dare to find out what secrets forests hold?

Plants through time

The first land plants appeared around 470 million years ago. These were mosses and liverworts, which grew close to the ground and had short roots. It took around another 80 million years for the first trees to grow. Between then and now, through planet-wide catastrophes and ice ages, plants have continued to change into what you see today.

Monkey puzzle tree

433 MILLION YEARS AGO
A plant with veins for carrying sugar and water around its body first grew. It had no roots or leaves.

Cooksonia

252 MILLION YEARS AGO
Ginkgos began to grow, including the biloba—a species still around today.

Gingko biloba

170 MILLION YEARS AGO
A unique, spiky Chilean pine appeared, which we now call the monkey puzzle.

395 MILLION YEARS AGO
The first trees appeared, with skinny, palmlike trunks, fronds at their heads, and spores instead of seeds.

33 ft (10 m)

Wattieza tree

251 MILLION YEARS AGO
The largest extinction event in history took place, wiping out 90 percent of life. It may have been caused by a huge volcanic eruption, which changed the climate and environment.

Modern magnolia

120 MILLION YEARS AGO
The first flowering trees began to grow. These were early types of today's magnolias.

80 MILLION YEARS AGO
Palm tree grew for the first time

360 MILLION YEARS AGO
Early ferns came into existence, with more and more types popping up, until ferns were one of the most common species of plant on Earth.

Fern

Mass extinction event

200 MILLION YEARS AGO
The first modern conifers grew.

Pine

Alamosaurus (a plant-eating dinosaur)

Palm

20

Meteor **CRASH!**

Earth

66 MILLION YEARS AGO

A huge, 6.2 mile (10 km) wide asteroid hit the Earth, causing MASSIVE devastation. Three-quarters of all plant and animal species became extinct.

THE OLDEST FOREST EVER DISCOVERED

In 2019, in a quarry in New York State, scientists discovered some fossilized roots. In fact, these were older than had ever been found before—they were from a forest that stood 386 million years ago.

60 MILLION YEARS AGO

The planet was filled with forests as far as the eye could see. The climate was much warmer than today—tropical plants thrived and deciduous trees, such as oaks, first grew.

2.6 MILLION YEARS AGO

Now began a series of ice ages (when most of the Earth was covered in ice). The last great ice age peaked 20,000 years ago. Global temperatures at that time were 20°F (11°C) colder than today.

Saber-toothed cats lived in the last ice age.

10,000 BCE

The last great ice age ended. The forests that had survived the cold covered 45 percent of Earth's land.

The climate began to cool.

But all was not lost. The plant-eating dinosaurs had gone. And the ashes of living things killed in the explosion gave the soil more nutrients for plants to use. The forests of plants that we know and love today began to spring out of the ground.

The cold weather affected plant life. Many forests disappeared, and tropical plants farther away from the equator died.

Methuselah

3,000 BCE

A bristlecone pine sprouted from a seed in California. Today, nicknamed Methuselah, it is the oldest known tree in the world.

1750 – PRESENT DAY

Machines for making goods first appeared in around 1750. Many of these, along with modern vehicles, make gases that cause the Earth's temperature to rise. This causes droughts, or long periods with no rain, and wildfires that kill plant life.

49 MILLION YEARS AGO

The first birch trees grew.

Axle

The wheel of fortune

In around 3,600 BCE, in Mesopotamia (which is now Iraq), the wheel was invented. It was a wooden disk that turned around a wooden axle. And it transformed life. Wheeled machines could prepare more soil, sow more seeds, and collect food faster. And transporting goods and people became far simpler, too.

Wooden disk

The age of wood

Human ancestors spent their lives swinging through trees. But for later human species, it was the trees' wood that moved to the center of life. It could be used to build fires, or carved into tools, weapons, and wheels. Eventually, it could be pulped and made into paper for communicating ideas and stories.

Marshmallow

Forest protectors

In the 18th century, the first forestry schools came into being to stop too many trees from being chopped down. They provided (and still do provide) expert advice and training for people who wanted to care for, or manage, forests—for example, by planting new trees.

Campfires burning

Homo erectus was the first human species to use fire. The burning wood kept them warm in the depths of their cave homes. It also left behind ashy traces for modern archaeologists to find one million years later.

The paper you are reading this on is from a managed forest. (Unless you have a digital copy!)

Before paper was invented, people would write on rough hemp sacks, rags, papyrus (made from a plant), wooden panels, and even animal skins. Pulp (wooden fibers mashed up) was first used to make paper around 200 BCE, though it took many centuries to develop the smooth, thin, pure white paper we now use.

One 46 ft (14 m) pine tree can produce 10,000 sheets of paper.

Strong oak and mahogany were the woods of choice for world-exploring European ships in the 15th century.

Ahoy, me shipmates

Wood has been used to build increasingly bigger boats for thousands of years. Wooden boats allowed people to settle on remote Pacific islands, and to explore every corner of the Earth.

23

La Lupuna

Respect must be shown to La Lupuna—a tall Amazonian tree. Its spirit is said to be the protector of the Amazon Rainforest. Beware if you chop down La Lupuna—it may take revenge...

The Silver Cat

In the USA, legend has it that there are large felines with a silver coat, red, burning eyes, spiky ears, and a solid, round "club" at the end of their tail, with spikes on one side. The cats sit in trees, waiting for victims—who they whack with their heavy tail before pulling them up to eat.

Moss people

German tales tell of magical wood folk who clad themselves in moss. They have a strong bond with the forests. Sometimes they are said to ask help from us humans—and to give wise words or bread as a gift in return.

La Sachamama, said to be the spirit mother of the Peruvian jungle, takes the form of a giant boa constrictor.

Folklore and fairy tales

For thousands of years, humankind has passed down stories of magical beings who lurk in the shadows of forests. Some of these look a little bit like real forest animals—but whether they're too big, too small, or with the addition of a magical horn, they're anything but ordinary.

BEAR WORSHIP

This famous, forest-dwelling animal might be real, but it is still at the heart of many supernatural stories. Early humans worshipped the bear in their caves, hoping to be helped in some way by the animal. Some North American Indigenous cultures have honored bears for centuries, as symbols of great strength and wisdom.

Enchanted

The use of magic wands by mythical witches and wizards can be traced back over 2,000 years. Made from wood such as rowan, elder, oak, or ash, these powerful objects focused the magic of their users during spells.

Robin Hood

This fabled outlaw lived in the depths of Sherwood Forest in medieval England. With his band of merry men, he stole from the rich to give to the poor.

Unicorns

It wouldn't be a magical forest without a unicorn! A mythical creature of beauty and goodness, the unicorn has captivated many different cultures' imaginations over the last 2,000 years. It is said to have lived in ancient forests, untouched by human hands.

Folklore and fairy tales continued...

The big bad wolf

This intelligent creature might be the ancestor of the cute, fluffy dogs that share human homes, but it has been cast as a villain in many a forest fable. The most famous is *Little Red Riding Hood*—in which the hungry wolf dresses as a grandmother to get close to a little girl he wants to gobble up.

THE BROTHERS GRIMM

From 1812, German brothers Wilhelm and Jacob Grimm published a collection of over 200 fairy tales. The stories featured magical beings in woods, inspired by the Black Forest in the brothers' homeland. Their stories were often retellings of older tales, passed down through time.

The Leshy

A defender of trees and tree-dwelling animals, the Leshy is a forest spirit from the Slavic regions of Europe. It is a shapeshifter—changing size and shape to trick people. You might hear it laughing or whistling in the depths of the forest.

Witches in woods

There are some who say witches lurk in the deepest and darkest woods, ready to snatch up victims to cook for dinner. In Romania, tales tell of Muma Pădurii—an old woman of the forests who LOVES to capture children and gobble them up for supper!

Fairies

Tales of fairy folk can be traced back thousands of years. There are hundreds of different types—some can be small, some rather tall, some quite friendly and some a little scary, and a few can even fly! Wood fairies live in splendid underground forest kingdoms.

Doon Hill

It is said that the doorway to a fairy realm can be found in an ancient pine tree in the woods of Doon Hill, Scotland. Over 400 years ago, a priest named Robert Kirk shared the fairy folks' secrets—so they trapped his spirit in the realm.

The little people

For many generations, Ireland has been a stronghold for fairy stories. The leprechaun is by far the most famous of all Irish fairies. Legend has it that if you are lucky enough to catch one of these tiny mischief-makers, he must grant you three wishes. Hurrah!

Hoia Baciu

Possibly one of the most haunted places on the planet, this creepy forest in Transylvania, Romania, holds many secrets. Ghosts have been spotted among the trees, and UFOs sighted overhead. Visitors have suddenly fallen ill, and there have even been disappearances. Enter at your peril!

Moose-pig

In the depths of the Forest of Dean, in England, once lurked the Beast of Dean. In the 19th century, this mysterious, boar-like animal was said to rampage through the forest. It gave off strange roars, and it was so big that trees in its path were knocked over.

FORBIDDEN FOREST

Just outside the Japanese city of Tokyo sits the bamboo forest of Yawata no Yabushirazu—which people are forbidden to enter. Some say that those who ignore the warning and step inside will be spirited away—which means taken to a spirit world.

Meooooow!

Bigfoot

Tall, apelike, and VERY hairy, this creature is said to live in mountainous forests in North America. It goes by many names, including Sasquatch, Yeti, and, of course, BIGFOOT—because of its MASSIVE footprints!

The Island of the Dolls

Tattered, grubby, spooky-looking dolls hang from the many branches on a small, wooded island just outside of Mexico City. A caretaker of the island began hanging them in 1950 to ward off the sorrowful spirit of a little girl who drowned nearby. Even today, the dolls' creepy eyes continue to watch from above.

The Jersey Devil

For the past 200 years, a legendary creature has lived in the Pine Barren Forests of New Jersey. It is said to look like a kangaroo, but with a horselike head, horns, and claws. Its call is a high-pitched, blood-curdling scream. AHHHHHHHHH!

Haunted and enchanted

The large, dark shadows of trees and the sounds of branches breaking under unseen animals' feet can make forests feel like the spookiest places to be. Tales through history tell of roaring beasts, grabbing ghosts, and haunted trees. There are plenty of after-dark frights in a forest at night...

Forests and humans

Cat chat

Cats have a much closer bond with humans than wild woodland animals do. They can recognize their owners' voices (and choose to ignore them)—and they only meow at humans, not at other cats!

Meow, meow, meow, meow

Throughout time, forests have provided humans with all kinds of important resources. There is wood for building things and pulp for paper. Forest plants and fungi were used as ancient medicines, and today many of the pills and syrups we need to fight diseases contain extracts (parts) of these organisms.

But some of the world's forests are in danger of deforestation, which is when they are cut down and not replaced, so that the land they stood on can be used for something else. When we cut down forests, it destroys the habitats of millions of animals. It affects the people who rely on forests to live. And it affects the climate of the whole world, because trees suck in gases that cause climate change. It's important to protect the forests that are left and to replace lost trees. We can all do our part to help our magical forests.

Henry Walter Bates
(1825–1892)

English explorer Henry spent 11 years making his way through the heart of the Amazon Rainforest. He made notes and drawings of the amazing insects and butterflies he found. That way he was able to share the wonders of the rainforest with the world.

Jadav Payeng
(1959–present)

The Molai Forest in India was planted by one person over 30 years—Jadav Payeng, also known as The Forest Man of India. Hundreds of species of animals now live among the forest's trees, including tigers, rhinos, and even visiting elephants.

LOST EXPLORERS

Dense forests have always been a magnet for adventurers keen to discover new plants and animals. However, some never return home. In 1925, the British explorer Percy Fawcett disappeared while searching for a lost city in the Amazon Rainforest. Many people who went to search for him were also lost—including his son.

Wangari Maathai
(1940–2011)

Kenyan Wangari began an organization called the Green Belt Movement, which helped communities in Kenya fight local deforestation. Her work has led to the planting of more than 30 million trees.

Fabulous forest folk

Over the ages, many environmentalists, scientists, and activists have dedicated themselves to defending the forests of the world. They have planted trees, protected existing areas, and spread the word about the importance of forests. Will you follow in their footsteps?

Margaret March-Mount
(c.1890—1950)

With one clever idea, Margaret helped plant more than 27 million trees! As a US Forest Service worker in the 1940s, she asked people to give money for planting in her "Penny Pines" initiative—which still exists today.

Alexander von Humboldt
(1769—1859)

Alexander explored the forests of continental America, finding unknown flora and fauna. He was one of the first scientists to say that animals and plants are all connected because they rely on each other for food and shelter.

Richard St. Barbe Baker
(1889—1982)

Founder of the International Tree Foundation, Richard was a forward-thinking early environmentalist. Nearly 100 years ago, he warned that losing our forests would worsen climate change. His greatest love? Planting trees.

Marina Silva
(1958—present)

A native Amazonian and a politician, Marina continues to fight against the deforestation of the Amazon Rainforest. She has helped to create protected reserves that are run by local communities. Go Marina!

Map of forests

No two forests are exactly alike. Trees might grow strange-looking features to withstand different weather, or they can become ultra tall to reach sunlight. Let's visit some of the world's most interesting forests.

Giant redwood

Rockefeller Forest

Boreal forests

The hottest

Beneath a huge glass dome in the Arizona desert sits Biosphere 2, the hottest tropical forest on Earth (though it was made by humans). It helps us learn the impact of climate change on rainforests. Temperatures can reach 104°F (40°C).

Biosphere 2

The tallest

Found within Humboldt Redwoods State Park in California, Rockefeller Forest is home to the towering, giant redwood trees. Among them is Hyperion, the tallest tree in the world.

The rarest

Monteverdi Cloud Forest is so high up in the mountains that it has clouds among the treetops! One of Earth's rarest habitats, it is teeming with life—including 500 species of birds. There are also many mysterious wildcat species.

Monteverdi Cloud Forest

Ocelot cats live in cloud forests.

Amazon Rainforest

The largest

The Amazon Rainforest is so big that it makes up half of our planet's remaining rainforest. It is one of the most important forests for controlling Earth's climate, as it has so many trees to absorb the gases that help cause climate change.

The odd-looking tapir lives in the Amazon.

The farthest south

On the southern part of Hornos Island is a chilly, windswept forest. It is so exposed to the wind that its trees have been changed. They are bent and short, only reaching around 10–13 ft (3–4 m). Taller branches or trees are simply blown over.

Hornos Island

Finland has the most trees in comparison to its size.

Russia has 642 billion trees—the most of any country.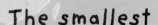

Boreal forests

The coldest

Boreal forests growing just below the Arctic Circle are our coldest forest habitats, with temperatures falling to −97°F (−54°C). As the world warms, some of these forests are moving even farther northward, to find the super-cold temperatures they are used to.

Crooked forest

The most crooked?!

A forest in northwest Poland is a top contender for the most-crooked prize. Here, a large group of pines have each grown in the shape of a J. Even more curious, the surrounding trees grow normally. Bizarre!

Socotra island

The weirdest

The island of Socotra is full of ancient dragon blood trees, which date back 50 million years. They look like umbrellas blown inside out—but even stranger, their resin, or sap, is the color of blood!

Dragon lood tree

KL Forest Eco Park

The smallest

Located within the city of Kuala Lumpur, in Malaysia, is the smallest rainforest in the world. KL Forest Eco Park is only the size of around 12 soccer fields. It is what's left of an ancient rainforest and is still full of life, despite being inside a bustling city.

Silvered leaf monkeys live in KL Forest Eco Park.

Daintree Rainforest

The oldest

The world's most ancient forest is thought to be 180 million years old. Daintree Rainforest has 30% of Australia's frog species, including the white-lipped tree frog, the world's largest frog! Ribbit, ribbit.

3 TRILLION!

Globally, there are approximately 3.4 trillion trees. That's 422 trees for every person on the planet! It may seem like a lot, but since humans have evolved, half of all trees have disappeared.

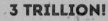

The graceful tree frog lives in the Daintree Rainforest.

35

City forests

Around the world, people are campaigning for cities to plant more trees and plan more parks. With climate change affecting us more and more, and now that we better understand the effect of green spaces on our health, it's important to fight for a greener future for our cities and towns.

Coyote

Clean, cool, and fresh

Trees clean the air of city pollution by taking in harmful gases. They can provide shade from the hot sun, or absorb heat to warm up an area. They can also absorb noise, block wind, and stop flooding by sucking up water from the soil.

Shady trees can reduce local temperatures by 5–9°F (3–5°C).

Planting trees near buildings can cut the use of air conditioning by up to 30% and reduce the use of heating by 20–50%.

Raccoon dog or tanuki in Japan.

Indian leopard

Forest cities

According to the United Nations organization, a forest is an area that is one-tenth trees or more, and bigger than 1.2 acres (0.5 hectares). This means that some cities are actually forests. London, UK, has around 8.4 million trees, making up 21% of its area—so, it's a forest!

New York City set itself a task in 2007 to plant a million trees across the city. They reached that goal and are now aiming to plant ANOTHER million by 2030. Nice job, New York City—and keep going!

Urban wildlife

City forests provide habitats for common (and not-so-common) animals and plants. Wild boar can be seen in many European cities, there are leopards in the Indian city of Mumbai, and coyotes live in Chicago, Illinois. In Tokyo, Japan, you might spot the shy raccoon dog called the tanuki. Wow!

Sloth in the city

In the sprawling city of Rio de Janeiro, Brazil, there sits an urban rainforest—Tijuca National Park. It's full of amazing critters. Three-toed sloths hang, snoozing from the trees, crab-eating raccoons go about their business, and bright red king snakes slither along branches. Sssssssss...

Tampa, Florida, has the most trees of any city worldwide, with 31% coverage.

Groundhog

Three-toed sloth

Nature's pharmacy

Nature can save lives. The ingredients of medicines can be found in forests, and especially in rainforests. These precious chemicals are often hidden inside fungi, or in the fruits, nuts, oils, and grains of plants. Medicines that come from forest life have been used to treat, or even to cure, diseases.

Under threat

More than 50,000 plants are used to make medicine worldwide. However, many of these are included in the 40% of plant life that is under threat from deforestation or climate change. In fact, our planet is losing plant species faster than scientists can discover and name new ones.

Fever tree

The cinchona tree is found deep in the Andean rainforests. This endangered tree's bark contains a medicine called quinine, which has saved millions and millions of lives from malaria—an often deadly disease carried by mosquitos.

People have been using plants to heal for thousands of years

Deadly arrow

Curare liana is a strong, woody, climbing vine of the South American forests. Originally, a poison taken from this plant was used by local tribes to coat the tips of arrows. The same substance has also been used by doctors to relax patients' muscles.

Cat claw

CLAWS!

In the tropical rainforest, you might spot what you think are cats' claws reaching down from above. In fact, these are giant, clawlike thorns on the vine of a plant called (of course) cat's claws. Scientists think it may help our immune system fight infections.

25%
of all Western medicines come directly or indirectly from rainforest plants.

Willow bark has been used for hundreds of years to treat aches, pains, and fevers.

MIMI

Palm oil blues

Huge areas of forests are being cut down to be replaced with oil palm trees. These trees make palm oil—a crop that is often used in things we buy, such as peanut butter and shampoo. But the old trees were the homes and food sources of many animals.

Wildfires

Hotter and drier weather due to climate change has caused a rise in wildfires. These fires rip through forests, destroying trees and leaving animals homeless. By taking actions to help stop climate change—for example, by using cars and planes less—we can do our part to help stop these fires.

Illegal activities

In many places, governments have created laws to stop too much forest from being chopped down. Unfortunately, criminals continue to cut down trees without paying attention to the law. It is up to local governments to stop this from happening.

Crops and cattle

All of the humans in the world need feeding. Huge amounts of forests are cleared to make way for fields that cattle, such as cows, can graze on—or to grow crops, such as soy, to feed the animals we eat. It takes much less land to grow crops for humans to eat than to raise animals, so eating less meat could help stop deforestation.

Trees in trouble

Humans have been cutting down trees for thousands of years. But as the population of the Earth has grown, so has the number of trees being cut down. Modern forests that are felled for wood or paper are usually replanted, but other areas of forests are being cleared and not replaced, often so that farm animals can graze. This could spell big trouble for our planet.

ONE TRILLION TREES

In 2006, a campaign to plant one billion trees was launched. In 2018, a new campaign began—this time to plant a trillion trees. There are movements across the world to help make this number a reality. But it is key to plant trees in the right places— and not to destroy important habitats to make way for them.

A forest the size of a soccer field is cut down every second.

2,400
trees are cut down every minute!

1,400
species of trees are critically endangered.

Animals in danger

In ancient habitats, even replacing old trees with younger ones can cause problems. Creatures there feed on the plants and animals around them, so if any one living thing can't survive in the new trees, this can affect the others, too. The answer? Protect the ancient forests we already have.

Orangutans could be gone from the wild in 30 years.

Better choices

Buying something with a "recycled" label means that old material has been used to make it. For wood, paper, or cardboard, this means no new trees were chopped down! You can also reduce what you use, or reuse.

Saving species

Protecting forests, plants, and animals is called conservation. Breeding programs (getting animals to have babies, or growing plants) help stop endangered species from becoming extinct.

Carefully does it

Some trees are cut down in a way that causes less harm to forests. New trees can be planted to replace those lost, or the ecosystem can be monitored to make sure it is still going strong. This type of tree felling is called "sustainable harvesting."

Powerful helpers

Globally, more than 14 percent of our land area is protected by governments, sanctuaries, and charities. Let's keep the pressure on those in power to keep protecting forests—and to keep adding to the list!

Check for a logo

It might be impossible to stop using paper—it's in packaging, books, and a lot more. But if a product has "FSC" (Forest Stewardship Council) or "PEFC" (Programme for the Endorsement of Forest Certification) on its label, then it comes from a sustainable source.

Helping forests

It's not too late to stop the disappearance of our wonderful forests and natural spaces. Governments can make the biggest changes, by protecting forests. But sometimes it's as simple as looking to see where the things we buy have come from, and making sure they're from forests that are being cared for. We can do this—together!

54 Commonwealth countries have committed to conserving 115 forest sites, covering nearly 30 million acres (12 million hectares). That's bigger than the country of Malawi!

Let's come together and protect important habitats!

Commonwealth areas

A royal canopy

In 2015, Queen Elizabeth II launched a project to protect the forests of countries in a group called the Commonwealth of Nations. Named the Queen's Commonwealth Canopy, the project covers nearly every continent on Earth.

Are you a forest helper?

Do you tell your friends at school and family at home how important forests are?

   a.   Yes
   b.   Sometimes
   c.   No

Do you check that food containing palm oil is made by sustainable sources?

   a.   Yes
   b.   Sometimes
   c.   No

Do you check if the FSC or PEFC logo is on the books you read and the paper you use?

   a.   Yes
   b.   Sometimes
   c.   No

Do you waste less paper by using both sides?

   a.   Yes
   b.   Sometimes
   c.   No

Mostly a's: You are a super-duper forest champion!

Mostly b's: With a little more effort, you can be a great forest supporter.

Mostly c's: After reading this book, you're well on your way to becoming a forest fanatic.

43

Forest habitats

Right or left?
Some animals, including the amazing species found in forests, can be left-pawed or right-pawed—just like humans! The same goes for cats, too.

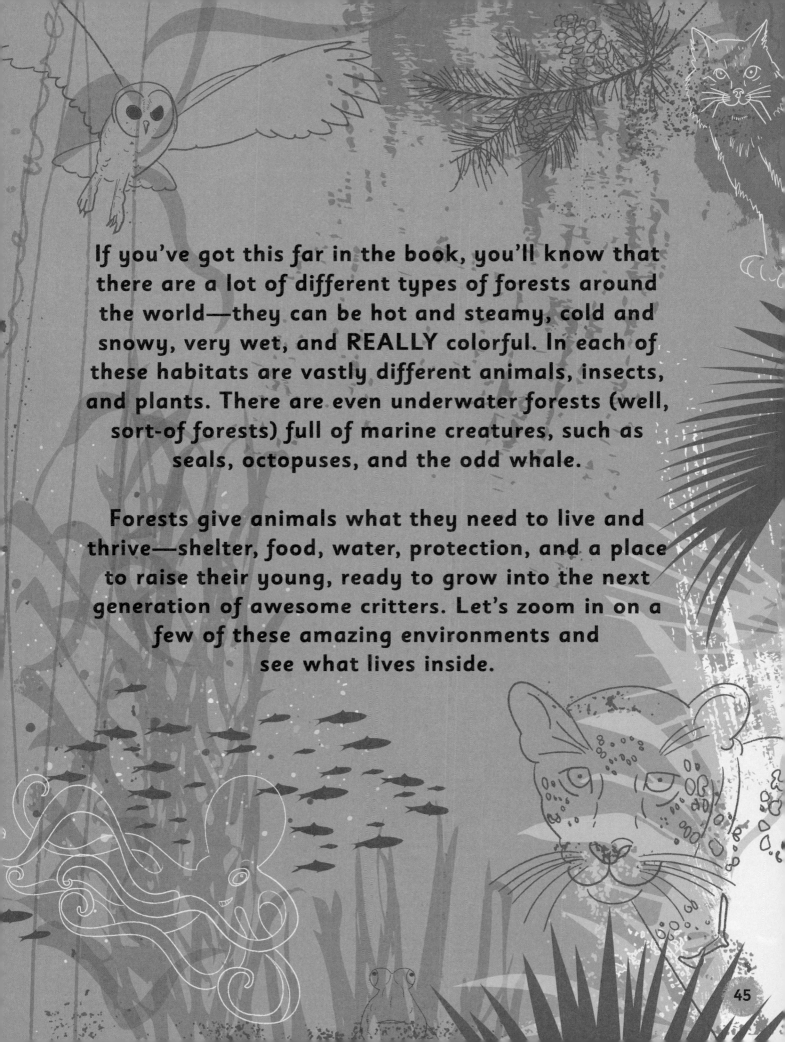

If you've got this far in the book, you'll know that there are a lot of different types of forests around the world—they can be hot and steamy, cold and snowy, very wet, and REALLY colorful. In each of these habitats are vastly different animals, insects, and plants. There are even underwater forests (well, sort-of forests) full of marine creatures, such as seals, octopuses, and the odd whale.

Forests give animals what they need to live and thrive—shelter, food, water, protection, and a place to raise their young, ready to grow into the next generation of awesome critters. Let's zoom in on a few of these amazing environments and see what lives inside.

FOREST FERN

One of the few plants that can grow under a pine tree is a fern. It's a plant that produces spores rather than seeds and flowers. Lady fern is one of over 10,000 different species of ferns—it thrives in the same sort of soil as pines.

Scoffing squirrel

There are 350 different squirrel types, but it's the red squirrel that LOVES pine trees. There are two types of red squirrels, the American and the European. American squirrels munch on pine cones. They throw the leftovers on a garbage pile called a midden.

Crossbill

Pine marten

Munching moose

Moose are herbivores, which means they eat plants—and they need to eat A LOT of those. They will munch on leaves, buds, pine cones, river plants, grass, and whatever else they can get their mouths on. In the cold winter months, when food is scarce, they can still eat pine needles, twigs, and bark to fill their tummies.

What lives in a pine forest?

Pines are often found in the far north, and are adapted to the cold weather there. They are a haven for birds and mammals that eat their pine cones and nest in their evergreen branches. Watch out for bears and wolves, too! AWWWWOOOOOOO!

Midden

Noisy woodpecker

These birds have strong, sharp beaks for loudly hammering holes in tree trunks, and a long tongue for reaching in to grab insects. They also like to lick at the tree sap. Slurp!

Pileated woodpecker

Great gray owl

Bounding bobcat

These excellent climbers roam the forests of North America and can often be seen up in the trees. They are around twice the size of house cats, such as Mimi, and have tufted ears. Their short, stubby tail looks like it's been cut, or bobbed—which is why they are called bobcats.

Boundless bark

Pine trees have thick, scaly bark that leaks a sticky resin or sap (which smells delicious). A lot of insects and spiders live in the cracks. When a tree dies, its bark continues to be home to many creatures.

Pine woods tree frog

Greedy grizzly

In the forests of Yellowstone National Park live big, brown grizzly bears. Not only do they love to fish in forest rivers, but they also like to snack on moths. Well, not really snack— one bear can eat 40,000 army cutworm moths in one day! Now that's just greedy.

Fern

Hedgehog mushroom

King bolete

What lives in a
mangrove forest?

In tropical, coastal saltwater areas grow groups of small trees and shrubs, called mangrove forests. The trees' long, gnarly roots sit above and below the water. The forests are home to all different kinds of plants and animals, and they protect the coastline from the ravages of the sea.

SALTY LEAVES

Mangrove trees take in salty water and expel the excess salt from their leaves. Their long roots create huge, nest-like structures, which are perfect for both land and sea creatures to live and feed in.

Limpkin

Spoon-fed

Shrimp eat algae containing carotenoids, which turn things pink. Roseate spoonbills eat the shrimp— which makes them pink! Using their long, spoonlike bill, they sweep through the water, collecting their food. Guzzle, guzzle.

Chomp chomp

Dugongs roam the seabed looking for sea grass, which is the only thing they eat. Surprisingly, their closest land relatives are elephants! Sadly, these wonderful creatures are endangered, partly due to lower amounts of sea grass.

Bluestriped grunt

Mangrove soil stores 10 times more carbon than rainforests.

Horseshoe crab

Mangrove tree crab

Hoatzin

Fruit bat

Snake eyes

Marsupials have pouches in which their babies grow. They also have long tails, strong toes, and REALLY furry coats. One example is the cuscus. Curiously, this cute-looking animal has pupils that are narrow, like a snake's! There are 26 types, and they live in Cape York, in Australia, and New Guinea.

Mangrove cuckoo

Perfect catch

Fishing cats lurk among the roots of the South Asian mangroves, on the lookout for tasty fish dinners. Twice the size of Mimi, they are expert hunters, diving into the water for fish or scooping them out with their webbed paws.

Mangrove monitor lizard

Mangrove trees are the only tree type that can live in salt water.

Mangrove snapper

American crocodile

Walking fish

With big, swiveling eyes and a long, pointed body, mudskippers are odd-looking fish. They also have an unusual talent—they can walk! Using their pectoral fins, they can climb out of the water. They are amphibious, meaning they can live out of water for extended periods of time.

Fiddler crab

What lives in an
ancient forest?

Areas of ancient or old-growth forests—that's woodland with trees that have been growing for hundreds of years—are excellent habitats for a large array of wonderful wildlife and plants. Mostly untouched by human activity, these environments take many years to develop into amazing ecosystems.

WHAT IS AN ANCIENT FOREST?

To be an ancient forest, the habitat must be mostly made up of large, old trees of mixed species, along with dead trees, either still standing or rotting on the forest floor. They might also be called old-growth, primary, primeval, or virgin forests.

Porcupine

Deadwood

A dead tree that still stands is called a snag. The tree may be dead, but it is still full of life—namely fabulous creatures, such as millipedes, centipedes, beetles, and snails. These make tasty grub for visiting birds and animals.

Song thrush

European badger

Not a cat

Fisher cats live in North American forests, and are around the size of house cats, such as Mimi. Despite their name, they do not eat fish (they prefer spiky porcupines), and they are not cats! They are more like badgers, otters, and weasels.

Bluebells

Bracket fungi

Stag beetle

Magpie ink cap

On the hunt

Northern spotted owls live in the ancient evergreen forests of North America. They only nest in old-growth trees. The owls hunt at night, peering through the gloom for flying squirrels and wood rats— their favorite dinner snack.

Raccoon

Flying squirrel

A cozy home

Older, decaying trees are home to 75 percent of animals that nest in trees. As a tree ages, holes appear in the trunks and large branches. These cavities make safe, cozy homes.

Back in time

Thousands of years ago, great forests covered Europe. Now, the last primeval woodland left is in Białowieża Forest, which sits on the border of Poland and Belarus. Untouched by humans for hundreds of years, bison, bears, lynx, and wolves still roam in this vital habitat.

Wolf

Big beasts

The European bison is the largest land mammal in Europe. Rewilding programs, which aim to bring back lost wildlife to an area, have rescued them from near extinction. There are now up to 7,000 of these magnificent beasts.

Wood rat

Red admiral

Cloud forest
pygmy owl

Toucan

Toucan birds make strange croaking noises, like frogs!

Masked
trogon

Sticky pads

Gorgeous, red-eyed tree frogs
are vivid green, with bright orange
hands and feet. Their colorful digits
have pads that ooze a sticky mucus,
which helps them grip onto
tree branches. Neat!

Resplendent quetzals

One of the most beautiful birds in the
world lives up in the canopy, eating
wild avocados, berries, insects, and
even frogs and lizards. But the quetzal
is endangered because its habitats,
such as cloud forests, are threatened.

Quetzel tail feathers can take three years to grow.

MASSES OF MOSS

Cloud forests are cooler than
tropical rainforests, as they are
higher up. This creates perfect
conditions for mosses and lichens
to grow. Mosses cover everything
from the ground up. They drip from
tree branches, creating a
magical-looking green world.

Western
mountain
coati

Tall tails

Coatis, or coatimundis, live in troops of
up to 30. When strolling on the ground,
they hold their tails up high, which
some scientists think helps them lead
the way for others. They also use
their tails for balance, as they
climb up high in the trees to
find the perfect nighttime
sleeping spot. Zzzzzzzzz.

What lives in a cloud forest?

High up in the mountains are tropical forests that have clouds forming at the tops of their trees. These humid, foggy forests are an extraordinary habitat, stuffed with wonderful wildlife and tangled plants. Exotic birds flit between the branches, and wildcats slink among the trees.

Spectacled bear

Magenta-throated woodstar

Coppery-headed emerald

Hummmmmmm

The hummingbird gets its name from the humming sound its wings make as they beat quickly up and down. This species is the only bird that can fly backward!

Olinguito

We rarely find brand-new species of mammals these days—but the olinguito was only discovered in 2013, in the cloud forests of the Northern Andes. It looks like a cute little teddy bear, and it can be seen leaping from branch to branch or snacking on figs.

Glasswing butterfly

Garden emerald

Big bite

Jaguars, the third-biggest cat in the world, have the most powerful bite of all cats. Their teeth are so strong they can bite through a crocodile's thick skin and crunch through the hard shell of a turtle.

Cloud forest parrot snake

Big eyes, small brain

Tiny tarsiers have really big eyes—so big that they are bigger than their brains! Tarsiers are a primate—that's a type of monkey species. They are so small that they can fit into the palm of an adult human hand. They come out at night and scoff insects, small lizards, and they can even snatch birds and bats.

ACTUAL SIZE

Rosy periwinkle

There are flying snakes!

Paradise tree snake

Blue morpho

Odd-looking

A tapir looks like a cross between a wild boar and a small elephant. Their long nose, or snout, is not only excellent at sniffing through the forest, but also perfect for grabbing fruits and leaves to feed on. One of the many ways they communicate with each other is by whistling. Phweeee!

Poison dart frog

Bird of paradise

What lives in a
rainforest?

Of all the forests in the world, rainforests support the most animals and plants. Lush, warm, and wet, they are teeming with mammals, reptiles, birds, and insects. So much life is packed into these dense habitats that scientists believe there are many species yet to be discovered. How exciting!

Goliath beetle

Vampire bats form lifelong friendships.

Blood drinker

A vampire bat's only source of food is mammal blood. They feast by cutting a small hole in the animal's skin with their sharp teeth and lapping up the pooling blood with their tongues. Slurp!

Forest gardener

Leaf-cutter ant colonies can contain more than 10 million ants. As their name suggests, the ants cut up leaves and take them underground to use in food gardens. They chew the leaves to a gloopy pulp, a fungus grows on top of the pulp, and the ants feed on the fungus.

Greater hornbill

Capybaras are calm, friendly, and sturdy—which makes them excellent perches for other animals!

Tropical kingbird

Squirrel monkey

Bananaquit

Long in the tooth

Capybaras are the world's largest rodents. Like all rodents, their teeth never stop growing. They must keep chewing on plants and tough bark to wear down their teeth and stop them from growing too long. Plants can be hard to digest, so sometimes they eat their own poop to absorb the food again. Ewww!

What lives in an
underwater forest?

Kelp forests can be found in cool, shallow waters off coasts around the world. They are not actually forests, as kelp is a type of seaweed, not a tree. This habitat is called a forest because kelp grow close together, like trees. And, just like in a forest, thousands of species live there.

KELP ANATOMY

Kelp has three parts. The holdfast is a mass of roots that anchors onto rocks or other things on the seabed, the stipe is the stalk, and the fronds are long leaves.

Wandering whales

Huge gray whales hang out in kelp forests, especially to hide from killer whales, who hunt them. Gray whales don't have teeth. Instead, they suck up food like a vacuum cleaner. Masses of white barnacles hitch rides on their skin, along with thousands of whale lice.

Common octopus

Clever camo

Superintelligent octopuses can change color when camouflaging—and they can even transform themselves to look like kelp fronds. Muscles under their skin inflate to create the illusion of rippled seaweed.

Wolffish

Speedy grower

Kelp can grow up to 12 in (30 cm) a day. Its fronds can become 100 ft (30 m) long—their length helps them to reach and capture sunlight, which they make into energy.

Sea urchin

Adorable otters

Cute sea otters are beneficial for kelp, as they stuff themselves on red urchins, which can spread too much and damage the ecosystem. Sea otters use the kelp fronds like blankets when they sleep on the surface of the water. Snuggly!

Gas-filled air sacs help the kelp to float.

Kelp rockfish

Freaky fish

There are 100 different types of rockfish, with many different colors and sizes. The kelp rockfish hangs upside down under the long fronds of the kelp. It has big eyes, a spiked back, and large lips.

Blue rockfish

Common or harbor seal

Olive rockfish

Snacking seals

With so many fish, kelp forests are a perfect hunting ground for seals and sea lions. The kelp forests also offer these marine animals excellent protection from predators.

Tiny invertebrates, such as snails and scuds, are food for all sorts of creatures.

Mind, body, and soul

purr... purr... purr...

The healing power of the purr

Forests aren't the only thing that's good for our well-being. The sound of a cat's purr can lower our stress and anxiety (worry) levels.

Forests can make you feel tree-mendous!
Just a couple of short walks in the woods a
week might improve your health—both mental
(your mood) and physical (your body). Walking
among the trees can reduce stress or make you
feel less tense. Some people even think that
just breathing in the forest air can boost
your body's immune system—which
fights off diseases.

What's more, forests are EXCELLENT places
to spot nature, which can be a wonderful way
to improve your mood. There are scurrying
mammals, chirping birds, buzzing insects,
beautiful flowers, diving amphibians, and
dramatic fungi (which are all worth a
trip by themselves).

True or false?

Is it true that forests can move? Do leaves change color and drop only in fall? Can insects disguise themselves as leaves? And are there REALLY trees that have been to the moon? Let's find out.

Trees block out noise.

True

Called attenuation, leaves and branches block out sound waves and deflect sound (which means they bounce it away).

Leaves change color and drop only in fall.

False

If a tree is stressed—which might be because of drought, disease, or insect pests—it can change color and drop its leaves as a defense.

Forests move!

True

Tree populations can actually migrate (move) across the landscape! If there are good growing conditions to one side of a forest, seeds will start growing there—until the whole forest has moved in that direction. But it's not quick—it takes centuries.

Insect or leaf?

There are more than 50 species of leaf insects. They camouflage (disguise) themselves to look exactly like leaves, and even sway in the wind.

MOON TREES!

Five species of tree seeds were taken up into space on the Apollo 14 mission in 1971. They orbited the moon and returned to Earth to be planted. Some are still growing today.

Over 50% of our total forest area is in just five countries.

True

The combined forests of Russia, China, the USA, Canada, and Brazil make up 54% of the world's forested areas.

There is a forest made up of just one tree.

True

In Utah, there is a forest that seems to have 40,000 trees—but they are actually just one tree with a huge, ancient root system. The tree is named Pando, or the Trembling Giant.

There are fewer grizzly bears in the USA now than there were in 1975.

False

Thanks to conservation efforts, such as stopping people from hunting bears, the number of grizzly bears has grown since 1975.

Hello!

61

Forest bathing for two

Breathing in scents released by trees and plants may improve your health.

Forest Bathing

This type of bath doesn't involve warm water or a tub. Instead, you are bathing in nature. As you stand among the trees, you might find that you feel less stressed or worried. Forest bathing might also improve your sleep, make you feel more creative, lift your mood, and improve your ability to pay attention.

SHINRIN-YOKU

In 1982, the Japanese government created the term Shinrin-Yoku—which means "forest bathing." The idea is to let nature into your body using your senses—such as seeing, hearing, touching, and smelling.

Science and nature

Scientists have discovered that spending time among trees seems to reduce stress hormones, such as cortisol, and can help improve physical and mental well-being.

Take a thoughtful approach to being in nature. hours a week may make you feel happier and healthier.

Let's relax

Tips for forest bathing

Turn off all electronic devices.

Walk as SLOWLY as you can through the trees.

Take long, DEEP breaths.

LISTEN carefully to the sounds of the forest. What can you hear?

SNIFF the air. What can you smell?

What can you FEEL? The breeze on your skin? The touch of a leaf?

Look around you. What can you SEE? Patterns in the canopy? Animals scurrying away?

It's also the perfect time for a picnic! You might notice that everything you eat tastes FANTASTIC!

Now take some time to just RELAX.

Mimi says, have an adult with you to keep you safe—and they will benefit, too!

Pine fresh

Not only do pine trees smell lush, but they may also have health benefits. They release vapors called terpenes, which can help with inflammation (swelling). When you walk through the trees and inhale the air, it might expand your airways and make you feel refreshed. Ahhhhhh...

Monarch butterfly

Health boosters

The forests are full of phytoncides—chemicals in the air that are expelled by plants to protect them against invading insects. When we breathe these in, they can trigger natural killer cells in our bodies, which get rid of infected cells. This helps our immune system to fight off infection.

Forest bumblebee

Free hugs

Hormones are chemicals inside our bodies that do different jobs. Oxytocin is a hormone that makes us feel relaxed—and hugging a tree can increase our level of this hormone. The hormones serotonin and dopamine, which make us feel happy, can also be increased by hugging. Go on, give a tree a cuddle!

Scientists have found that the most relaxing colors are greens and blues.

Orange-tip butterfly

Just looking at trees can lower blood pressure and improve mood!

CO2

A breath of fresh air

Trees absorb nasty air pollution, which can harm us if we breathe it in. So, green spaces with a lot of trees in towns and cities are important for our health.

VIRTUAL FOREST

In scientific experiments, even looking at pictures of forests can be good for us. A beautiful image of a forest causes changes in our bodies and brains that make us feel more relaxed.

Wren

Tweet tweet

Birdsong not only sounds wonderful, but some scientists have found that it can help us to relax. Early morning bird tweeting might even stimulate our brainpower! The birds can help with homework.

Mind and body

Hugging trees, listening to birdsong, or simply standing and breathing in the forest air might have health benefits, whether helping your body to fight infection or making you feel calm and happy. Hospital patients have even been known to recover a little quicker with a forest view! Hurrah!

Tree bumblebee

Indoor

Ready to
put in the
ground

activities

Grow an oak tree

Collect some acorns and take off the little caps.
Place the acorns in water—if they float, discard
them. Plant a nonfloating seed in a small pot of
soil and water it frequently. Be patient—it can
take a few months for the seedling to appear.
When it is taller than a pencil, place it in the
ground and watch it grow. What a tree-t!

Oak seedling

Remove
acorn cap.

You could
draw faces!

Acorn

Draw a tree from memory

Think of trees that you have seen.
Can you remember the shape of
their leaves, or if they were wide
or narrow? Try drawing one—or
invent your very own tree!

Make some leaf art

Collect some leaves and flatten them
between the pages of a book—you
could even use this one. When the
leaves are flat, draw around them on a
piece of paper or cardboard to create leaf
outlines. Then fill them in how you like.

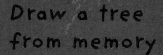

Collect some little sticks on your next walk.

Create a stick flag!

Pick a stick from your collection.
Fold a piece of paper in half to make
a rectangle. On both sides of the
rectangle, draw a design. Place your
stick on the inside fold, and glue the
rectangle together. You now have a
fabulous flag to display or wave!

Rectangle

Outdoor
activities

Build a den

Ask a parent or guardian to help with this one. Collect some big sticks and lean them carefully against a tree trunk or low, thick branch, to create a den.

Mimi says make sure it's safe before getting inside.

String

Sticks

Decorate with leaves and moss.

Make a woodland fairy house

Fairies also love dens! Collect some little sticks and lean them against each other to make a mini tent. Tie string or long grass around the top where the sticks meet to secure it. Add camouflage with leaves and pine cones. Ta-da!

Bark rubbings

For this, you'll need paper, crayons, and some interesting tree bark. Hold the paper against the trunk of the tree and rub the long end of the crayon against the paper. Then, watch as amazing patterns appear. Label it with the tree's name, if you know it!

Go on a sound safari

Listen to the rustling leaves. Can you hear some buzzing bees? Chirping birds on branches up high? Animals snuffling quite close by? There's a lot to be heard among the trees. Forests really are magical!

After all that exercise and fresh air, you'll sleep like a log!

Glossary

AMPHIBIAN
Animal with a spine, cold blood, and moist skin, which is able to live either on land or in water, and which lays its eggs in water. Frogs are amphibians

CANOPY
Ceiling of treetops in a forest

CARBON
Substance found in all known living things on Earth. It can turn into a gas called carbon dioxide (CO_2), which helps cause climate change

CLIMATE
Usual weather conditions for an area

CLIMATE CHANGE
Change in temperature and weather across the Earth, which can be natural or caused by human activity

CONSERVATION
Act of protecting forests, plants, and animals

DROUGHT
Long period of time without rain

ECOSYSTEM
Animals, plants, and other living things in an environment that rely on one another to survive, for example for food or shelter

ENVIRONMENT
Area in which an animal, fungus, or plant lives. A forest is a type of environment

EQUATOR
Imaginary line around the Earth, between the North and South Poles

EVOLVED
When a species of animal, plant, or fungus has changed over a long period of time, sometimes into a new species

EXTINCTION
When a species of living thing dies out

FELLING
Another word for chopping down trees

FOREST
Area with a lot of trees

FUNGUS
Living thing that is neither a plant nor an animal, which has a body made up of a network of threadlike hyphae. Some fungi have fruiting bodies called mushrooms

GAS
Substance with no fixed shape that expands to fill the space it is in. Air is made up of different gases

HABITAT
Place where an animal is suited to living. Forests are a habitat for a lot of different animals

HORMONE
Chemical inside your body that has a certain effect, such as making you feel happy

HUMID
Type of weather that is damp with water droplets in the air, and usually hot

IMMUNE SYSTEM
Parts of your body that work together to fight off illness

JUNGLE
Unmanaged forest with many tangled plants and a lot of layers of canopy

LEAF
Part of a plant that absorbs sunlight, made green by a chemical called chlorophyll

MAMMAL
Animal with warm blood, hair or fur, and a spine, which makes milk to feed its young. Squirrels are mammals

MANAGED
When a forest is taken care of by humans. Planting new trees when old ones are chopped down is a way of managing a forest

MARINE
When an animal, plant, or fungus lives in water

NUTRIENTS
Substances eaten by plants, animals, and fungi that help their bodies to stay healthy

OXYGEN
Gas that almost all living things need to take in to stay alive

POLLUTION
Harmful substance in the air, soil, or water

RAINFOREST
Forest with a lot of rainfall

ROOT
Part of a plant that takes in water, usually from soil

STEM
Part of a plant that usually holds up leaves and flowers, through which water and nutrients are transported from the roots to other parts

SUSTAINABLE
When something can be used for a long time, or replaced easily

VAPOR
Gas that has come from a liquid being heated or squashed enough, such as water vapor

WOODLAND
Managed area of forest, which has less canopy cover than other forests

Index

2004-2019

Mimi
(Tree hugger)

Vicky Woodgate

2004-2021

Moka
(Leaf sniffer)

About the author

Vicky Woodgate shared her life with two VERY special life teachers, Moka and Mimi. They are the inspiration for our forest guide Mimi cat. Vicky continues to write and illustrate more books from the sunny south coast of England. She lives on top of a hill with her husband, Bert the garden hedgehog and his girlfriend, plus three snoozing slow worms.

For

The BEST parents EVER
Mum, Ray, Dad, and Alison xxx

My friend Lou Gardiner, a forest lover,
and a tree hugger x

There are 62 acorns in this book. Can you find them?

Acorn

DK would like to thank the following:
Polly Goodman for proofreading, Helen Peters for indexing, and Sakshi Saluja for picture research.

The publisher would like to thank the following for their kind permission to reproduce their photographs:

(Key: a-above; b-below/bottom; c-center; f-far; l-left; r-right; t-top)

20 Dreamstime.com: Tetyana Korop (cb); Ncl (cra). **Getty Images / iStock:** ilbusca (t, b). **Shutterstock.com:** Nenov Brothers Images (ca). **21 Dreamstime.com:** James Mattil (bc); Vaeenma (bl). **22 SuperStock:** Science Museum / SSPL (tl). **22-23 Dreamstime.com:** Serjio74 (c). **23 Dreamstime.com:** Andreykuzmin (tr). **25 Dreamstime.com:** ç€ åå. **Getty Images / iStock:** hokmesso (ca). **26 Alamy Stock Photo:** Matthew Corrigan (cr). **Shutterstock.com:** Olga_i (tl). **27 Alamy Stock Photo:** Charles Walker Collection (clb). **Dreamstime.com:** Oleksii Bernaz (bc). **Mary Evans Picture Library:** Medici (cra). **28-29 Shutterstock.com:** Squeeb Creative (t); Stone36. **29 Shutterstock.com:** Jakub Krechowicz (tr). **32 Getty Images / iStock:** ilbusca (l). **32-33 Getty Images / iStock:** Hein Nouwens (c). **33 Getty Images / iStock:** ilbusca (bc, tc, cr). **61 Getty Images / iStock:** dzika_mrowka (tr); Alan Owen (cla). **62-63 Shutterstock.com:** Yarygin. **64 Alamy Stock Photo:** Leon Werdinger (c). **64-65 Shutterstock.com:** Yulik_art (t)

All other images © Dorling Kindersley